UNDERSTANDING AND LOVING SOMEONE WITH PTSD

PTSD Self Help Book

John Anikpo

CONTENTS

PREAMBLE
UNDERSTANDING TRAUMA
SIGNS OF TRAUMA
STRATEGIES FOR HELPING SOMEONE WITH TRAUMA
CONCLUSION

PREAMBLE

Post-Traumatic Stress Disorder (PTSD) is a complex and often misunderstood condition that affects millions of individuals worldwide. Characterized by a range of symptoms, including intrusive thoughts, avoidance behaviors, and heightened arousal, PTSD can have a profound impact on an individual's life, relationships, and overall well-being.

Supporting and understanding those impacted by trauma is extremely difficult in a situation where memories of past suffering continue to come and go. People who experience trauma often have complex and multifaceted effects that make life challenging. However, understanding can act as a beacon, showing the ways in which we can assist others in recovering and growing.

The purpose of this book is to enable us to understand the concept of trauma, its symptoms and triggers, and how we can support ourselves and others in many ways. With an understanding of the various aspects of trauma, such as PTSD and C-PTSD, we gain more insight into what people are experiencing on a deeper level. This positions us well to be of help at the best level we can.

The book makes it easier to understand how a person's life can be impacted by past trauma and the issues that may arise as a result. It also instructs us on how to interact with those who have suffered trauma. Through frank and compassionate communication, we get better at listening to their problems and emotions without passing judgment, which makes them feel heard and supported.

When reading along, we see how trauma can cause some people to withdraw or isolate themselves. We learn to accept their need for space while simultaneously providing support, and we also learn why they do this. Avoidance is yet another typical trauma-related reaction. We come to understand that people have the right to stay away from things that trigger memories of their trauma while also giving them the confidence to confront their fears when the time is right. We also examine other aspects of trauma, such as hypervigilance and rigid thinking, throughout the book. As we provide support based on empathy and compassion, we gain the ability to be patient and understanding.

Altogether, it's a fundamental aspect of PTSD, aiming to provide you with essential insights and tools to better understand and support those grappling with this condition. Whether you are a friend, family member, caregiver, or healthcare professional, gaining a deeper understanding of PTSD can make a significant difference in how you approach and assist someone who is going through this challenging journey. By offering practical guidance and insights, we hope to empower you to become valuable allies in the recovery and healing process for someone living with PTSD as well as yourself.

UNDERSTANDING TRAUMA

A traumatic experience is an occurrence that leaves a person feeling powerless and horrified. The vast majority of us, at some point in our lives, have been exposed to some kind of traumatic event about anything.

A traumatic injury, on the other hand, is the result of the repercussions of that trauma on a person's mental, emotional, psychological, and social relationships with others. Unresolved trauma may lead to severe injuries that are more widespread and more permanent than they would otherwise be.

It is critical that we recognize that not everyone who is exposed to trauma will acquire PTSD or cPTSD. Similarly, not everyone who has a physical injury will have complications or long-term issues as a consequence of the accident. Some individuals recover completely, although a large number of others may have negative effects.

Chronic or continuous traumatic stress and the variation in stress perception between children and adults are often ignored or downplayed in the conventional concept of trauma. The PTSD diagnostic criteria don't seem to do a good job of defining trauma, which is a problem because most people associate trauma with extremely horrible events, but chronic stress from things like a dysfunctional family or a traumatic event in childhood can also manifest in subtler ways.

Therefore, it is essential to keep in mind that the definition of trauma varies from person to person. The individual experienced feelings of helplessness and dread at the moment of the traumatic event, if the event was ever distressing. When compared to a person who is 22 years old, a child who is just two years old will experience a distinct kind of trauma.

There are a number of instances in which people who have experienced trauma are either misdiagnosed as having another condition or the diagnosis is overlooked entirely. It is very important that trauma be handled, and it is possible that they have both the disease and the trauma. Whether it's physical trauma and they're medicating pain or psychological trauma and they're medicating distress, a significant number of individuals who struggle with addictions are self-medicating their trauma with substances. It is not uncommon for people who are addicted to feel certain things when they are addicted. In the treatment of addiction, this is yet another aspect to take into consideration.

Attention deficit hyperactivity disorder (ADHD) is yet another example of a diagnosis that is either overlooked or incorrectly made. PTSD and chronic post-traumatic stress disorder (cPTSD) are both characterized by symptoms such as trouble paying attention, difficulty concentrating, impatience, and restlessness. In light of this, it is imperative that the history of the individual be investigated: when did these symptoms first appear? Do you have to decide whether you are dealing with anything like chronic post-traumatic stress disorder (PTSD), attention-deficit/hyperactivity disorder (ADHD), or both?

In addition, according to the International Classification of Diseases 11 (ICD 11), a person should not be given a different diagnosis if the criteria, which are the symptoms of chronic post-traumatic stress disorder (CPTSD), adequately describe what is going on with them. However, if it does not provide a complete explanation of what is occurring, then one needs to investigate if there are other diagnoses that may be applicable.

It's possible that people who suffer from anxiety, whether it's generalized anxiety or social anxiety, have been through traumatic experiences. The question that we want to ask is, What is the cause of that anxiety? The question is if it was brought on by the fact that the person was raised in a family where there was domestic violence or where there was a significant amount of rejection (for example, pathological narcissistic parents who were consistently rejecting).

Due to the attachment trauma, bipolar illness, and depression that the individual has experienced, they have a great deal of anxiety when they are in the company of other people in their adult life. In this book, we will open our minds to bipolar disorder, which is a very frequent symptom or outcome of having experienced trauma, feeling hopeless and powerless, and being unable to alter the situation.

Being unable to recuperate and feeling despair is a fairly frequent experience. It's common to have a great deal of guilt. You may also experience hypomania or mania if you have bipolar disorder. The condition known as hypomania is particularly fascinating to examine since it often occurs when a person is feeling energized yet does not want sleep. There is a possibility that this is an indicator of hyperactivation of the stress response system, which is the HPA axis, which is telling us that it is not safe to sleep and that we should remain awake.

Generally speaking, a diagnosis of bipolar disorder is likely to be made if the individual in question exhibits hypomanic signs or, more specifically, manic symptoms. On the other hand, we must acknowledge that there is also the possibility of a diagnosis of trauma, and if we do not treat everything, the individual will not be able to make the most of their rehabilitation.

Both attachment problems and personality disorders are characterized by the same symptoms. In order to answer this question, we need to examine the symptoms. Which message is being sent here? Was there a traumatic event that led to the development of this pattern of behavior? Do you think that the child developed this pattern of behavior as a means of protecting themselves in a setting that was very chaotic, stressful, and frightening, and in which they did not know what was going to happen from one minute to the next? OR was concerned about their safety and whether or not they would be catered to. You should realize that it is quite obvious that this would be considered traumatic neglect. Both purposeful and inadvertent negligence are possible at this point. It is possible for a caregiver to neglect a child if they are so preoccupied with their own responsibilities that they fail to notice the child. They are unable to find out how to solve their own problems. They are hardly capable of functioning on their own. They are unable to provide for the requirements of the youngster. You might also have a more intentional situation in which the caregiver does not care about the child, does not want the child, or neglects the child for their own personal advantage.

Consequently, we see instances of abuse, neglect, and abandonment, which may occur as a result of death or divorce. There is no way for us to know for certain whether we are going to live or die. This is something that is inherently impossible. Despite the fact that we do not want to place blame on the individual who passes away as a result of a heart attack, it is nonetheless very distressing for a kid to face the realization that their primary caregiver is no longer around. "In the event that my other caregiver suddenly disappears again, what are the consequences?" They may ask. What a terrifying thought! Should I be prepared for this? Is it possible that I will just abandon my presence here? This is for a child who has had the experience of being abandoned.

When it comes to a child, they could even blame themselves for what took place. In spite of the fact that they could be quite furious about what occurred, the child is going through a highly painful experience.

Additionally, in certain cases, things end up going better when the caregivers split; it's simply that it's genuinely better. This is the case with divorce. In spite of this, the child's life has evolved. The child's life has been altered, and they did not have any choice in the matter. They are no longer living in the same home as both of their parents. It is possible that the kid would experience feelings of abandonment, shame, and the belief that it is their fault, even if the situation is for the best.

When there is a person in the home who suffers from a mental illness or addiction, and if that person is a caregiver, they are often unable to be as attentive, caring, and consistent with the kid, which may result in attachment trauma. In situations where it is someone else, such as a brother or sister, for instance, the caregivers are often so preoccupied with trying to cure that individual that they fail to see what is going on with other children at that time. As a result, there is a possibility that a certain level of negligence occurred. However, in general, we take into consideration this unintentional neglect. They are not attempting to ignore a youngster who is in good health. They have no intention of ignoring the youngster for their own personal gain. It is just that they are unable to refer to or concentrate on that individual.

All of these things have the potential to cause trauma. And it emphasizes the importance of properly investigating history to fully understand the root of each trauma.

SIGNS OF TRAUMA

1. Are you agitated or irritable?

Many times, people who have been through traumatic experiences feel agitated or irritable. They are so anxious that they are excessively attentive. Due to the fact that they do not feel secure, they are always on edge. Concentration deficit hyperactivity disorder (ADHD) is characterized by a number of executive functioning issues, including impulsivity and concentration problems.

How does this relate to a traumatic experience? For those who are really watchful, this is a state of hypervigilance. If you are continually looking around the room to make sure that you are secure — you are the kind of person who does not feel comfortable — you are going to have a difficult time paying attention to the arithmetic problems that are written on the board before you or the spreadsheet that you are working on.

When you are in a state of hypervigilance, you are in fight-or-flight mode. It will be more challenging to find a solution to an issue if you are experiencing trauma or a lack of a sense of safety. If someone is in a fight or flight state, the ability to solve problems is at the very bottom of the list. Keeping you safe is the objective of the fight-or-flight strategy. Therefore, executive functioning is put on the back burner for the time being. That's a kind of traumatic state we should also watch out for in people. It could stem from their past experience with insecurities, past unsafe situations, or a potential hazard that's still recorded in their mind.

2. Sensitivity to impulses

People who have been through traumatic experiences tend to be very alert. Additionally, if you are strolling through a haunted home, for instance, you should worry about yourself. You are really watchful, you are looking at everything about you, and you are waiting to have a look at what is going to manifest itself. Then there is the moment when something does emerge. As a result, you react, and your reaction is impulsive. You are making an effort to safeguard yourself because, all of a sudden, that danger is there in front of you. You are being impulsive.

People who have experienced trauma in the past may be more impulsive, and they may respond in a more emotional manner. This is often due to the fact that they are thrust into the fight or flight zone so completely that they are attempting to defend themselves.

3. Dysregulation of Emotional States

Emotional dysregulation is another symptom that may be caused by traumatic experiences. In the event that you have an emotional reaction and you believe that there is anything that occurs that most likely merits a reaction of level 2, but you replied with a level 9, nonetheless, this is an example of a hyper-emotional reaction. So, in your perspective, you had an excessively powerful emotional reaction when you were in that circumstance—it's because your hypothalamic-pituitary-adrenal (HPA) axis is dysregulated.

Also, individuals who have been through traumatic experiences may develop a condition known as glucocorticoid resistance—a condition in which the cells of the body gradually become less responsive to the effects of glucocorticoid hormones, such as cortisol, or become resistant to those effects. Different physiologic functions, such as metabolism, immune response, and stress response, are all regulated by glucocorticoids, which play an important role in the regulation of these activities. The most essential note is that they often have a feeling of being flat; they don't feel a lot of stuff. Simply put, they are attempting to make it through the day. On the other hand, when something does occur, people who have not been traumatized experience a trickle of stress hormones that assist them in coping with the situation throughout the movie. When a person who has experienced trauma goes from having not much to a flood of stress hormones, they are like, "Alright, we know what to do here, we are going to bolt into action." This is often a learned response.

In essence, we are saying the extreme emotional reaction that persons who have emotional dysregulation experience could be at the high end, low end, or just includes explosive fury as one of its components. Those who have been through traumatic experiences often feel uncomfortable. One of the ways in which we react when we feel uncomfortable? Anger!

4. Inner Anger

Anger is one of the reactions that may be given to threats. The fact that they desire to push it away, get rid of it, and dominate it is evidence that they are continuing to act on impulses. People who have been through traumatic experiences may have more explosive rage and may feel as if they have a more difficult time coping with it because they are reacting from a place that is based on the perception of something being a danger if the traumatic event occurred while the individual was a youngster.

All the same, we acquire a great deal of coping skills whenever we go through any kind of traumatic event, regardless of whether or not the kid went through the same thing. It is possible that they had a more concrete way of thinking, and it is also possible that they did not have the emotional coping ability repertoire that we hope adults come equipped with. To put it another way, when someone is feeling threatened, we could see that inner kid emerge (even when the person is now a grown-up adult). And the child's explosive rage, which they had been using as a kind of self-defense while they were in that chaotic setting, bursts out.

5. Challenges in the Management of Emotional States

Individuals who have experienced trauma are characterized by inadequate appraisal resolution and control of unpleasant emotional states, according to the findings of another study that I discovered. In other words, that's a lot of nonsense, if you ask me.

To put it simply, if you have been through a traumatic situation, it is not at all improbable that you will have trouble recognizing how you are feeling. Simply put, you act and respond. The labeling of those feelings and the evaluation of events to identify what constitutes a danger and what does not constitute a threat are both obstacles that you struggle with. You basically react to everything as if it were a danger, you know what I mean? The resolution of that emotional reaction is difficult for them to achieve. It is well known that individuals who are emotionally dysregulated react more strongly to stress and need a longer period of time to return to their baseline for the purpose of resolving that emotional reaction than those who have not experienced trauma. In addition, they struggle to control unpleasant emotional states in any situation. They have a difficult time ending that pattern once they have begun what they are doing. This fight-or-flight reaction has been activated as a result of them. And depending on the time period in which the traumatic event occurred or the degree of the trauma, the individual may not have acquired sufficient coping skills to assist them in resolving or managing the unpleasant emotional state that they are experiencing. It's possible that they don't have a vast array of reaction possibilities at their disposal. It is important for us to keep this in mind.

6. Low levels of motivation and apathy

Apathy, or a lack of drive, is another way that trauma manifests itself. Many individuals will have feelings of self-doubt due to the fact that they lack a significant amount of motivation. As a result of their feelings of depression or apathy. They are just not very concerned with it.

One of the symptoms of post-traumatic stress disorder (PTSD) is emotional numbing, which is also often referred to as a muted aspect or, once again, apathy right out of the study. This psychological state may act as a barrier to motivation. People who have been through traumatic experiences may be unable to fully feel the effects of the trauma because they find it too frightening or uncomfortable. Simply put, they do not want to experience any feelings because they are terrified that if they did, they would be unable to stop themselves from experiencing them. It's also possible that the HPA axis is dysregulated, and they are just too weary to feel anything. The exhaustion is too much. They have no interest in anything. Essentially, you'll hear,

"I don't have it in me anymore. I simply don't have it." It's lost — the feeling, passion, love, or anything else that it may be.

7. Mood disorders

There are a number of symptoms that are related to sadness; however, the manifestation of depression itself is that sense of being blue or having a poor mood.

Chronic and recurrent exposure to stress has the effect of impairing the HPA axis's ability to function properly. This is something that has previously been discussed, and it is a factor that leads to the development of major depressive illness. It is common knowledge that prolonged exposure to stress may result in the development of symptoms of depression as well as post-traumatic stress disorder (PTSD). One of the primary reasons for this is the dysregulation of the HPA axis. Cortisol is continually hammering at the door, saying, "Hey, we need to be awake." This happens when a person has been under stress for a significant amount of time. At some point, the door stopped opening, and the corpse spoke the following: "You know what? Unfortunately, I am unable to answer the door at this time.' It starts becoming impossible to cope with it. At this point, this phenomenon was previously referred to as glucocorticoid resistance. In the event that this occurs, however, it indicates that the individual will also have problems experiencing any joyful feelings. This is due to the fact that pleasure and excitement are also components of the HPA axis. Not only will the individual not experience as much anger or fear, but they will also not experience as much pleasure or exhilaration as they might, if the body is unable to react to excitatory neurochemicals. This means that the individual will not feel as much as they could.

8. Avoiding People or Getting Attached to People

When people have been through traumatic experiences, particularly if they acquire post-traumatic stress disorder (PTSD), but even if they have not, if they have what is known as sub-drama or not yet diagnosable PTSD, this does not imply that it does not have an impact on the person. People who have been through traumatic experiences and who continue to feel unsafe and powerless are likely to be far more scared than those who have not. When a person is afraid, when they do not feel secure, when they do not feel powerful, they are going to have a tough time relaxing, and they may even have trouble being independent at times.

A number of individuals who have been through traumatic experiences are in severe need of having someone else there to safeguard them; some need their space to feel secured. These people who have been through traumatic experiences, or those who have been on the other end of the spectrum, have little need for other people since other people were the source of their suffering in the first place. Therefore, not everyone has the same level of hardship when they are alone. However, it is essential to ask oneself, What function is this serving? Does it come to any of your behaviors or any of your symptoms? When did it first become apparent? What are the many ways in which it may have evolved in order to assist me in remaining safe?

People who suffer from post-traumatic stress disorder (PTSD) may have avoidance symptoms that last for longer than a month. On the other hand, we often link such avoidance with triggers that remind us of the traumatic experience. There are going to be a lot of reminders of the trauma that you had as a youngster on account of the fact that you grew up with traumatic events.

Although avoidant or anxious attachment is not uncommon, it is important to note that if the trauma in question is attachment trauma, then connecting to any person might potentially elicit that stress reaction. It is possible that certain individuals will possess a lack of use for the majority of people, and this may be due to the fact that individuals wore the precipitator precipitators of that trauma. This is also true for withdrawing from social situations. There are situations when it is possible that the trauma is caused by other individuals. On the other hand, there are times when being in situations where there is a lot of activity is just too stressful for one to handle. Suddenly, the individual's hypervigilance meter goes off the charts, and they feel as if they are completely overwhelmed. Therefore, there are a great many different ways in which harmful things might manifest themselves.

9. High sensitivity to interpersonal relationships

This is not a standard sign of post-traumatic stress disorder (PTSD), but high interpersonal sensitivity is another one of those things that we don't speak about very often with one another. A significant number of people who have been through traumatic experiences, particularly attachment trauma, have a tendency to have a high sensitivity to rejection. Just like when we discussed hypersensitivity to one's environment, the feeling that people get here is that they have to walk on eggshells every single time in order to avoid being punished by the rejection or desertion of other people. Therefore, their existence is characterized by the fact that they are hypersensitive to every micro-expression that individuals make by being hyper vigilant to everyone that is in their immediate vicinity. And part of this may also be in an attempt to make sure, quote unquote, that they've got someone there to assist them since they were abandoned when they were unable to take care of themselves.

Therefore, the high level of interpersonal sensitivity serves as a safeguard against potential harm. Then there is the phenomenon of sensory hypersensitivity, which refers to those who are more sensitive to noises, scents, and sights. It has been shown by researchers that individuals who suffer from post-traumatic stress disorder (PTSD) may experience a plethora of sensations, and that those who suffer from PTSD and also experience PTSD also have what is known as poor sensory gating.

Moreover, one of the symptoms of attention-deficit/hyperactivity disorder (ADHD) is inadequate sensory gating. Interesting enough, there are also those who suffer from schizophrenia. However, what this really means is that the brain has trouble distinguishing between things that are essential and things that are not important, and it simply becomes overwhelmed with every sight, scent, sound, and smell that is present in the surroundings. This may make it difficult to pay attention. In addition, those who have been through traumatic experiences may also be hypersensitive to specific reminders of the trauma they have encountered.

Individuals that have the appearance of the perpetrator, odors, rejection, or abandonment, tend to bring back memories of the traumatic experience or event.

It could be something you may not think of; it could be noise! It is possible that individuals may become hypersensitive to noises from one point of a bad event, for instance, if the fire alarm was the one that alerted them to the fact that their home was on fire. And that panic reaction is triggered each and every time there is a sound that even closely resembles a fire alarm. We just have to understand where every traumatic experience is coming from, and it'll be very easy to help ourselves or someone else.

10. Autoimmune disorders and degenerative diseases

There is also a clear correlation between trauma and the development of illnesses and autoimmune diseases. A dysregulated HPA axis, also known as the stress response system, is a consequence of trauma, which has an inextricable effect on the immune system. During the first phase, which occurs in the immediate aftermath of the trauma, the immune system is repressed. What does that tell us? Suppressing the immune system allows the body to concentrate its energy on either fighting or fleeing from the threat. The immune system, on the other hand, will ultimately tell you, "Hey, we need to send out our workers to repair anything that's breaking down." This will happen if the stress continues to persist. This results in an increased level of immune system activation. The immune system begins to send out workers in an effort to repair all of the damage that was done while they were waiting for the shock to pass, and this process continues even after the trauma has passed. This is the beginning of systemic inflammation.

There is a reciprocal relationship between immune system malfunction and trauma, as well as traumatic stress symptoms. There is an increase in inflammation throughout the body once the immune system begins to function at an elevated level. It has been shown that an increase in inflammation is linked to an increase in anxiety and depression, and that an increase in anxiety and depression stimulates even more stress, which in turn activates even more of that immune system.

11.   Heart and Blood vessel disease

There are a number of biological changes that may be brought about by traumatic injuries. These changes include increased activity on the HPA axis, reactivity of the autonomic nervous system, inflammation, oxidative stress, and endothelial dysfunction. These changes have the potential to contribute to the development of cardiovascular problems, both with and without chest pain.

There are certain people who are going to have that awful chest pain, but not everyone who is suffering from a cardiac episode will have it. On the other hand, they discovered that those who have been subjected to chronic continuing stress and chronic trauma have a great deal of alterations in their microvasculature.

12.   Issues with Sleeping

This may be one of the few symptoms. However, circadian misalignment is quite frequent in post-traumatic stress disorder (PTSD) and glucocorticoid resistance, which is any trouble with the body's response to cortisol. Beginning with the waking response cortisol, which is at its greatest in the morning and then gradually drops during the day, the circadian rhythms are able to function in part because of this. If, on the other hand, your body is no longer reacting to cortisol, then your circadian rhythm will get thrown off since none of the other systems will be able to tell whether you are thinking that your body is a factory. No one in the remaining departments is aware of the times at which they are expected to report to work and the times at which they are expected to leave for the day. Therefore, this is associated with dysregulation of the neuroendocrine, immunological, metabolic, and autonomic systems, as well as disruptions in sleep. One study found that people with post-traumatic stress disorder (PTSD) had a much higher rate, regardless of their physiological weight. The most important takeaway is that they have a much greater incidence of sleep apnea, in addition to insomnia, which may result in difficulties getting asleep or remaining asleep after falling asleep.

Many individuals who have been through traumatic situations could not even be aware of it since it was those traumatic events that occurred throughout childhood. It was a truly terrible setting in which they were raised. In addition, our culture does not often consider it to be a painful experience. The situation is terrible, but it is not traumatic. Yet, we need to begin labeling it as traumatic so that others can comprehend the physiological effect that it had on the kid and the person who experienced it. It is possible to trace the origin of many symptoms back to either the formation of behavior in order to live or the outcome of physical changes brought on by dysregulation of the HPA axis. It may be helpful for those to plan a more successful rehabilitation process if they are aware of the ways in which a chaotic upbringing, unfavorable childhood experiences, and chronic stress may directly lead to symptoms that are experienced in the present day.

STRATEGIES FOR HELPING SOMEONE WITH TRAUMA

Now that we have a better understanding of trauma, the causes, and the symptoms of post-traumatic stress disorder (PTSD) and chronic post-traumatic stress disorder (cPTSD). In the framework of this discussion, it will be a means of determining methods to provide assistance to the individual and to cope with their symptoms, as well as to investigate the ways in which their symptoms affect us and to devise methods for self-care.

1. Communicate With Them

It is essential to speak with the person who is experiencing any or all of these symptoms in order to provide support for them. It is also necessary to discuss with them their vulnerabilities, triggers, and the solutions they have found (if any).

Why is it important to know about their vulnerabilities? It is because we are sure to keep in mind that vulnerabilities are things that increase the likelihood that they may be activated. For instance, if they have been through a traumatic event and it occurred in a public setting, then it is possible that they are already more primed when they are in circumstances that include public settings. Certain individuals are more susceptible to being triggered or to having these symptoms activated in them because they are vulnerable at that instance.

Similarly, if the issue happened at home, then when they are at home by themselves, they may be more susceptible to experiencing some of these symptoms.

In addition, it is essential to speak with them and inquire about the solutions that work for them. It is possible that the solutions that work for one (the supporter) are not the same solutions that work for another. Therefore, one has to inquire about the treatments that have been shown to be effective for the case at hand in order to manage the issue properly.

2. Understand Their Partial Need for Withdrawal and Isolation

If a person has gone through a traumatic event, particularly at the hands of other people who have victimized them in some manner, then they may withdraw from other people or isolate themselves since being around other people is as traumatic for them. It is possible that it is difficult for them to feel comfortable and at home with other people because it reminds them of the traumatic experience or because they do not trust other people.

On other occasions, they may withdraw from others or isolate themselves simply due to the fact that they are overstimulated and overwhelmed the majority of the time since they do not feel secure. It's not the fault of those around them; simply stated, they are unable to accept any more feedback. Asking your loved one about it is a good idea. Which of the following functions does withdrawal serve for you? Are you finding that it is helpful because you just cannot take any more, you feel overwhelmed, and you have no more input, or is it because being around people causes you to feel uncomfortable because you simply do not trust others, and this causes you to feel uneasy? Talking with them about that, and then when you have to go into situations that they would hurt or to withdraw from talking about ways to mitigate that, such as taking a ride on the bus, going shopping, or being home at night by themselves, or whatever it is that tends to make them feel comfortable,.

3. Avoidance of reminders

Additionally, this may occur along with withdrawal at times. If you have been through a traumatic incident: when you walk into a shop, travel to other locations, or watch different television programs, you may be reminded of that trauma. For the person who has experienced trauma, avoiding such reminders helps them feel secure. However, for the person who is in a relationship with them, they may feel as if they are being confined in some way because they are unable to do this, they are unable to do that, they are unable to watch this, etc. In order to assist a person in feeling secure, there is a comprehensive list of things that can and cannot be done. You should be aware of their preferences. — Take into account the fact that they may not want to watch certain things or visit certain locations. The reason for this is not because they are attempting to be harsh but because some locations are excessively triggering, and they also produce an excessive amount of worry. In the event that you have to go there, you can have a conversation with them about what you can do or what has to take place in order to make them feel safer or more powerful there. For instance, if they have been through a horrific experience at a hospital and are required to go to the hospital for some reason, I will speak to them about what I can do. "I am aware that you have had a really negative experience in the past; how is it that I am able to make it through this circumstance?"

Asking questions is the first method of communication that may be used to grab the other person.

It is also quite normal for people to have inflexible thinking as a result of having experienced trauma, and when those memories are aroused, they go into a fight or flight response. In the state of "fight or flight," individuals are not thinking; rather, they are responding and reacting to their surroundings. Because of this, thinking becomes rigid, and they are thinking things like, "I need to get out of here as soon as possible." This may come off as combative or unable to compromise. Is this person attempting to be oppositional, difficult, or argumentative, or are they stuck? This is something to consider while taking a step back and asking the question. There is a possibility that they are unable to think of anything else at this moment since they are locked in the fight or flight phase. Moreover, after they have reached their smart mind, they are able to participate in higher order thinking, which often results in a greater degree of flexibility. Or, at the very least, they may learn to be more receptive to considering new ideas. There is a possibility that they do not have any further recommendations, alternatives, or instruments that may be used. Therefore, they are treating every issue as if it's a nail since the only instrument they have at their disposal is a hammer. So, you can make them **feel safe** by avoiding those who remind them of the nails they once marched on.

4. Help them Feel safe

When you are in a state of "fight or flight," your stress response system is activated. Because of this, you won't be able to recall things, and this will also make it more difficult for you to focus. This might manifest itself in the form of inattentiveness when it is eaten. For instance, if the person does not feel comfortable and you are in a restaurant, they can be gazing around at everyone else. The reason is not that they are looking at other people or that they are not interested in you for some reason. One possible explanation is that they do not have a sense of security, and as a result, they are keeping a watchful eye out for any sign that things are about to go awry.

It is important to recognize that there are some circumstances in which it is more challenging for them to focus, as well as circumstances in which it is simpler for them to concentrate. If they are required to be at a restaurant, for instance, where do they feel safer? Are they more likely to feel secure if they are seated in a position that allows them to view both the entry and the exit, as well as the fact that they are up against a wall, as a lot of people do? In such a situation, they can sit facing the wall as opposed to facing the entry and exit doors. In people who have gone through traumatic experiences, hypervigilance is a highly prevalent trait. On the other hand, exercising extreme vigilance ensures that they will not be taken by surprise. When there are a lot of predators in the environment, being very watchful is similar to being a rabbit or a squirrel, which are both animals that are prey. In other words, individuals have trouble resting because they never feel completely and completely secure. It results in a chain reaction of difficulties all at once. Working with a person who has endured a traumatic injury would require that you pay attention to what they have to say about the circumstances on the ground, try to empathize with them, and think of ways in which you may assist them in feeling secure in it, as well as in achieving a state of relaxation, at least under certain conditions. Suppose, for instance, that they have a great deal of anxiety when driving, in which case you could drive and they could ride. There are other situations in which people could experience a great deal of stress if they are not driving. In such cases, you could help them by choosing to ride and they driving.

Another example may be when one is sitting outside. In the event that you go out, what would make them feel more secure? Perhaps it would be beneficial to avoid going to places that are really crowded or to visit parks at a time when they are less busy. Consequently, there are a variety of compromises, and this does not imply that you are required to be at home all the time. This is just to tell you to make the necessary preparations and have a reduced number of potentially stressful stimuli.

Hypervigilance may lead to tiredness as a result of its effects. And the persistent sense of being in danger due to the fact that the individual is often unable to obtain a decent night's sleep. Consider this scenario that worries one about having the windows open at night. If they can't see out, but what is outside can see them, then it doesn't work for them. What is it that you can do to feel secure in that house? Shut the blinds! At night, covering the shades helps them feel safer in my surroundings, which in turn lessens the amount of stress they experience.

There is a statistically significant link between experiencing a severe injury and the development of sleep apnea. If you're not sleeping well, it's crucial to have that examined. You are not going to be able to heal your stress response system, or the individual is not going to be able to heal their reaction, until they're able to obtain appropriate quality sleep. If you are a caregiver and they are waking up with night terrors, it is also important to recognize that their sleep difficulties are affecting themselves. In order to maintain health and function, as well as to recharge the life batteries, what steps can you take to ensure that they obtain a restful night's sleep? Well, you may not be able to address all of that. If you are able to, however, give them a heads-up before anything that might potentially surprise them and affect their rest. The severe stress reaction that occurs when one is shocked (despite the fact that it doesn't last very long) releases a significant amount of energy that can be stressful for someone healing from similar traumatic shock. To be of help, you should install customized closures on the doors of your cabinets so that they shut gently rather than slamming the same thing on all of the other doors in your home. Prior to making loud sounds, such as turning on the blender, you should wait. State that there is "loud noise." These are little things you can do to express compassion and kindness in a straightforward manner. It is possible that they were raised in a home where there was domestic violence, and as a result, they tend to raise their voices when other people start screaming or when they are becoming angry. At this point, they begin to experience a great deal of stress. In this case, naturally, it is essential to refrain from yelling in their presence. It is possible that they will be triggered if anything occurs to you that causes you to shout, such as if you drop something on your foot and it hurts extremely badly and then you yell all sorts of expletives. Assuming that this is the case, you should confront them and say, "You know, I'm sorry, I didn't mean to scream, everything is okay." Immediately addressing it may be helpful in reregulating them a little bit and urging them to assess the circumstances in which they are currently operating. At this particular moment in time, what did it imply in this context? Did you hear me scream? Let them know the screaming situation is not the same as it was twenty years ago, when they were at home and their caregiver began to yell.

5. Be Sensitive to their symptoms

There is also a high prevalence of physical symptoms in those who suffer from PTSD. There is a strong correlation between traumatic damage and a variety of symptoms, including systemic inflammation, teeth grinding, muscular tension, an upset stomach, and even autoimmune disorders.

It is possible that the individual who has been through traumatic experiences may have a greater number of physical symptoms, and those physical symptoms may become much more severe in proportion to the degree of stress or danger that they feel.

It is essential for us to be attentive to this, and once again, we must refrain from accusing them of hyperventilating in any manner. However, we must acknowledge the physical symptoms that they are experiencing, connect with them, and show as much compassion as we can.

Indeed, it is okay for you to find it aggravating and frustrating. Given that your significant other had a horrible night, you could have wanted to go hiking or you might have wanted to go do anything for the day, but your significant other was plagued by terrors throughout the night, and now that they are fatigued, they just do not have the energy to go and do it. We understand how this may be quite annoying, but show respect for the fact that they are worn out. Think of methods by which you might reach a solution that is acceptable to all parties. In certain cases, this may require you to go and do the task by yourself since they want to remain at home and relax and recoup. On other occasions, it may suggest that you alter your plans or that you are still going to do something together, but it may not be as active or for as long as you had originally planned. Have sympathy and acknowledge the traumatic experiences.

A person who has had a severe injury may also be impulsive because they are under stress and respond in an effort to shield themselves from the situation. These impulsive behaviors may include drinking, spontaneous shopping, or spending. To help with this situation, the surroundings and the circumstances that lead your loved one to be more prone to impulsivity are going to be vital to take into consideration. If you come out in a lot of different ways, it may be helpful to distract them from the pain or discomfort that they are experiencing, or it may be as a response to something they are seeing as a danger.

6. Acknowledge Their Feelings and Roots

Those who have suffered catastrophic injuries often have a more pessimistic outlook on life. This is due to the fact that after experiencing a traumatic event, they become very cautious since they are always looking for any indications of danger in their surroundings. Those who are hypervigilant tend to focus on the bad, while you, on the other hand, fail to see the good. Guess what? If you seek it out for a decent amount of time, you will eventually discover it. You can be sure that you will begin to have a more pessimistic outlook on life if you are constantly noting the bad aspects of the situation.

It is essential to acknowledge what individuals see and the views they have about the world. Invalidating their understandings and reactions is not a productive strategy. In the event that the person is happy with it, you have the option of presenting your own information or presenting more information. If they are in a situation in which they are seeing everything as bad, it is important to accept this with them first rather than telling them, "Hey, you ought to be enjoying this." Do not tell them what they ought to or ought not to feel on their own. They have the ability to recognize the things that are causing them worry, and you have the ability to let them know about the things that you are pleased with.

A significant number of individuals who have suffered severe injuries tend to numb themselves because the emotions they are experiencing are just too intense and overpowering, causing them to feel nothing at all. One unfortunate consequence of this is that it might be difficult for them to even consider the possibility of experiencing anything in the future. These people do not experience any feelings that are associated with the traumatic event; nonetheless, they struggle to feel anything about anything. Although this might be quite distressing for them, it can also be extremely frightening for them to even consider the possibility of beginning to feel because they are scared that if they do begin to feel, they will become emotionally overwhelmed again.

It is essential to refrain from "shoulding" those who have experienced emotional trauma, since doing so is equivalent to taking away their power by telling them that they should feel this way or that they shouldn't feel this way. By validating how they feel recognized, which means admitting it, you are not saying that you agree with them; rather, you are stating that you notice that they are stressed out, and you are discussing with them what it is that you can do to be as helpful as possible at this time.

Now, the reverse is dysregulation, which is when individuals move from being in a sort of flat state or maybe even a numb state to being in a state of wrath or franticness. When someone goes from being calm to being enraged or from being calm to being frenzied, it might seem like an overpowering situation. They may have the impression that they were standing on the beach when, all of a sudden, a tidal wave totally swallowed them, and it may take them a minute or even longer to regain their composure.

Even though whatever incident occurred only justifies a response of a three or a four, they are responding with a ten. They are not purposefully being unduly dramatic, yet at the same time, they are not exaggerating. They are really having a neurochemical response that is far more intense than that of someone who does not have a traumatic injury, someone who does not dysregulate. The reason for this is because, in contrast to the individual whose home flooded little due to the rupture of a pipe, this situation is more comparable to that of a person whose home flooded six feet deep due to the rupture of a dam in the town. The damage is far more severe in them, and it takes a significantly longer amount of time for the water to dry out. So do not scream that they screamed; they screamed because they're feeling it from a mindset entirely separate from yours.

7. Be Patient with Help

People with PTSD have felt a sense of powerlessness. If they have been subjected to persistent stress, particularly trauma that has lasted for years, then they may begin to feel powerless. In order to alter anything, help them to determine what it is that constitutes a life that is full and meaningful to them, what are the things that are causing them problems and causing them to be bothered. Helping them perceive these baby steps, or gradual improvement, might make them feel more powerful and give them the impression that they are safe in their existing setting. Please always remember that they are not going to change overnight.

8. Build Personalized Toolbox

Every person's version of trauma is a little bit different, and there is no one approach to helping those who have post-traumatic stress disorder (PTSD) or for people to see PTSD. In the end, we want to assist them in experiencing a sense of safety and the empowerment to maintain their own safety while also moving towards a life that they perceive to be full and important. On the other hand, its manifestation is going to be diverse for approximately every single individual. In order to assist people in feeling secure or powerful, it is essential to have a fundamental understanding of their vulnerabilities, triggers, and successful solutions.

When they are triggered, this will help you to have a toolbox that you can share with them, and they will have a toolbox that they can take from. This may be useful in encouraging conscious awareness of vulnerabilities and triggers. For instance, the holiday season is drawing near, and for some individuals, traveling home for the holidays is a time when they are surrounded by people from all different groups. With our understanding, people may suffer a much-increased sense of vulnerability during this time period because they could continually be reminded of the terrible events that occurred in the past.

In order to experience the highest potential level of safety and strength, we have come up with a toolbox! At least once in the morning and once in the evening, we are being encouraged to check in with ourselves by asking them, "What do you need right now?"

9. At Last, Take Care of Yourself

For you, when you are in a relationship with someone who has been through a traumatic situation, it is very important for you to take care of yourself. You will get exhausted and less able to empathize with others if you do not have any support for yourself. It is not going to be possible for you to be as caring and helpful as you might be if you take some time out for yourself to avoid the things that may lead to burnout occurring.

CONCLUSION

We've gone into great length on how trauma can truly upend our bodies, causing problems with our minds. Though it's a serious subject, understanding it is crucial if we are to help those who are going through difficult circumstances. Priority should be communication; we have to be willing to listen intently to what others have to say and open those channels. It's important to know where they're coming from as much as to hear what they say. Sometimes all it takes is someone to speak to.

Also, another important fact is that trauma affects the body as much as the intellect. Those bodily distresses are genuine and may be detrimental; they may manifest themselves as anything from heart issues to sleep difficulties.

It is so crucial that we look after ourselves on the inside as well. Not to be overlooked while discussing self-care is self-care. We cannot pour from an empty cup, so, schedule some alone time for yourself, whether it be a nature walk, a bubble bath, or just curling up with a nice book.

Trauma victims are among the toughest individuals on the planet, despite all they have experienced. They have persevered in the face of some difficult circumstances in ways that merit admiration. Therefore, the lesson from their endurance is that trauma doesn't have to define us. We are able to support one another in healing and moving ahead. No matter what they've experienced, everyone may feel appreciated and supported in a world we build together.

Recall also that it's OK not to know everything— not one of us does. We can, however, improve the lives of others around us if we are prepared to listen, learn, and lend a helping hand. Let us thus continually be there for one another, for where the magic occurs is when we really experience what someone else is experiencing and put ourselves in their position. Consequently, keep in mind to be nice when someone confides in you about their tragedy. Understanding will always involve action as well as emotion, so be prepared to provide settings where people feel comfortable telling their tales without fear of being judged or criticized. Consciously, we can dismantle those stigmas and prejudices and redefine how trauma is discussed in society.